About KET Practice Tests Plus

- KET Practice Tests Plus contains four Practice tests. These cover all the Papers of the examination. Each test is exactly the same format and is at the same level as the exam.

- Tests 1 and 2 offer a Preparation section for each Part of the exam. The exercises in this section take students step by step through the rubrics and task in each Part, so that they have a clear understanding of what they will meet in the exam and how to approach each task.

- The Preparation sections also offer grammar, vocabulary and communication exercises. These focus on language that is often tested in the exam and enable you and your students to see where further revision work is necessary.

- The Speaking Paper in Tests 1 and 2 provides structured preparation and oral practice. The Speaking Test must be taken by candidates in pairs and the exercises provide the opportunity for paired practice.

- There are additional practice exercises at the end of the Students' Book, which give the opportunity to revise some of the key areas of language covered in the four Tests.

- The Teacher's Notes in this book give further information about each Part of the exam, as well as suggestions for using the preparation exercises.

- There are photocopiable Answer sheets on pages 30–31 of the Teacher's Book. We suggest that you give students regular practice in transferring their answers to the Answer sheet.

Introduction to KET

KET (Key English Test) is based on the Waystage 1990 specification, or what may be achieved after approximately 180–200 hours of study, about half-way to PET (Preliminary English Test). It includes Reading, Writing, Listening and Speaking components.

The KET syllabus is designed to ensure that the test reflects the use of language in real life. The question types and formats have been devised with the purpose of fulfilling these aims. KET corresponds closely to an active and communicative approach to learning English, without neglecting the need for clarity and accuracy.

Assessment

T0344054

The three papers in the KET Reading and Writing component carries 50 per cent of the final marks. The Listening and Speaking components carry 25 per cent each. The final mark a candidate receives is an aggregate of the marks obtained in each of the three Papers. There is no minimum pass mark for individual Papers.

KET has two passing grades: **Pass with Merit, Pass** and two failing grades: **Narrow fail, Fail.**

'Pass' normally corresponds to about 70 per cent of the total marks. 'Pass with merit' corresponds to about 85 per cent of the total. A 'Narrow fail' means the candidate is within five per cent of the pass mark.

Paper 1: Reading and Writing (1 hour 10 minutes)

Component	No of Parts	Total mark for each component
Reading	5	40 ⎫
Writing	4	20 ⎭ 60 weighted to 50

Paper 2: Listening (approx. 25 minutes)

	No of Parts	Total mark for paper
Listening	5	25

Paper 3: Speaking (8–10 minutes)

	No of Parts	Total mark for paper
Speaking	2	20 weighted to 25

Paper 1, Part 8, Question 56

One mark is given for each question in Paper 1 and 2, except for Paper 1, Part 9, Question 56. This is marked out of five.

Mark	Criteria	
5	All three parts of the message clearly communicated. Only minor spelling errors or occasional grammatical errors.	
4	All three parts of message communicated. Some errors in spelling, grammar and / or punctuation.	
3	All three parts of the message attempted. Expression may require interpretation by the reader.	Two parts of the message are clearly communicated. Only minor spelling errors or occasional grammatical errors.
2	Only two parts of message communicated. Some errors in spelling and grammar. The errors in expression may require patience and interpretation by the reader.	
1	Only one part of the message communicated.	
0	Question unattempted, or totally incomprehensible response.	

© UCLES

Candidates are penalised for writing fewer than 25 words, but they are not penalised for writing more than 35 words, though they are not advised to write too much.

Assessment of the Speaking Test

The Speaking Test involves two examiners and a pair of candidates. One examiner is an interlocutor, while the other is an assessor and takes no part in the interaction. Candidates are given marks by both examiners. Candidates are not expected to produce completely accurate or fluent language but are expected to be able to interact appropriately with the interlocutor and each other. Assessment is made on the basis of:

- interactive skill.
- ability to communicate clearly in speech.
- accuracy of language use – grammar, vocabulary and pronunciation.

Both examiners give each candidate a mark out of 5 for each part of the test, giving a possible total of 20. This is weighted to a final mark of 25.

Language specifications

Key functions, notions and communicative tasks

- Introductions and greetings
- Asking for and giving personal details
- Understanding and completing forms
- Describing people: *personal appearance, qualities*
- Asking for and giving the spelling of words
- Counting and using numbers and telephone numbers
- Buying and selling things: *costs and amounts*
- Asking and telling people the time, day and/or date
- Talking about what people are doing at the moment
- Talking about past events and states in the past, recent activities and completed actions
- Understanding and producing simple narratives
- Talking about future situations, plans and intentions
- Making predictions
- Following and giving simple instructions
- Understanding simple signs and notices
- Asking the way and giving directions
- Asking for and giving travel information
- Identifying and describing simple objects: *shape, size, weight, colour, purpose* or *use*, etc.
- Making comparisons and expressing degrees of difference
- Expressing purpose, cause and result and giving reasons
- Making and responding to simple requests, offers and suggestions
- Giving and responding to invitations
- Giving advice, warnings and stating prohibitions
- Asking / telling people to do something
- Expressing obligation and lack of obligation
- Asking and giving / refusing permission to do something

- Making and responding to apologies and excuses
- Expressing agreement and disagreement
- Expressing preferences, likes and dislikes
- Talking about feelings
- Expressing opinions and making choices
- Expressing needs and wants

Topics

- Personal identification
- Personal feelings, opinions; personal experiences
- Hobbies and leisure
- Sport
- Travel and holidays
- Transport
- Health, medicine, exercise
- Shopping
- Clothes
- Services
- Language
- House and home
- Daily life
- Entertainment and media
- Social interaction
- School and study
- Food and drink
- People
- Places and buildings
- Weather
- The natural world
- Work and jobs

Lexis

The KET vocabulary list includes items which normally occur in the everyday vocabulary of native speakers using English today. Candidates should know the lexis relevant to their personal requirements, e.g. nationalities, hobbies, likes and dislikes.

More detailed information about KET language specifications may be found in the KET handbook available from the University of Cambridge Local Examinations Syndicate.

Teacher's guide and answer key

Note: There are photocopiable answer sheets on pages 30–31 of this Teacher's Book. You can use them to familiarise students with the format. Encourage them to write their answers in pencil on the exam task, then give them time to transfer these to the answer sheet after checking.

TEST 1

PAPER 1   Reading and Writing

The Reading test is divided into five parts. Reading texts are authentic texts, adapted where necessary so that most of the structures and vocabulary are known to students at this level. However, students are expected to be able to use guessing strategies if they meet unfamiliar structures or vocabulary.

Part 1, Questions 1–5

Teacher's Notes

In Part 1, candidates are tested on their ability to understand the main message of a sign, notice or other short text, such as a label from a food packet or bottle. The texts are normally authentic or semi-authentic. They may contain unfamiliar vocabulary but this should not inhibit learners, who will need to learn how to guess meaning from the overall context.

This is a matching question, requiring candidates to match five sentences to the appropriate sign or notice.
For questions 1–5, candidates have to match signs, notices or short texts with the correct explanation. There are two extra signs which candidates do not need to use.

PREPARATION

- Students read the instructions and the example to find out what the task is about.
- Point out that signs are often about things you *can, can't, must* or *mustn't* do. Exercise 3 focuses on the use and meaning of these verbs in signs.
- Remind students to use the clues to help them with the exam task.
- Tell them to write their answers in pencil on the task.
- Encourage students to explain their answers to the task.
- After checking answers, you can tell students to transfer their answers to the answer sheet.

PREPARATION   Part 1 Key

Exercise 1
1 'Which notice says this?'
2 Five questions.
3 On the answer sheet.

Exercise 2
1 can't smoke   2 (here)

Exercise 3
a 〉 1 can't, 2 must, 3 can't, 4 must, 5 must
b 〉 1 can't, 2 can, 3 must, 4 can't, 5 can, 6 mustn't, 7 can, 8 can't, 9 must, 10 must

EXAM PRACTICE   Part 1 Key

1 D, **2** G, **3** A, **4** B, **5** F

Part 2, Questions 6–10

In Part 2, candidates are tested on their reading and on their ability to identify appropriate vocabulary. Candidates read six sentences (including one integrated example) with a connecting link of a topic or a storyline. For each of the five questions, there are three-option multiple-choice answers. Prepositions will not be tested in this part of the exam.

PREPARATION

- These exercises practise the type of language found in Part 2.
- Encourage your students to produce their own six-sentence stories, similar to the ones in this part of the exam.
- Make sure students read the instructions and the example carefully before doing the exam task.

PREPARATION   Part 2 Key

Exercise 1
1 Paula and Maria going to a basketball match.
2 Five questions
3 On the answer sheet

Exercise 2
'decided' is followed by 'to'

Exercise 3
1 decided, 2 met, 3 walked, 4 enjoy, 5 wanted

Exercise 4
1a ticket,	b cheque,	c money
2a already,	b ever,	c yet
3a group,	b team,	c player
4a felt,	b decided,	c thought

EXAM PRACTICE   Part 2 Key

6 C, **7** A, **8** B, **9** A, **10** C

Part 3, Questions 11–15

Teacher's notes

In Part 3, candidates are tested on their ability to understand the language of the routine transactions of daily life. For each question 11–15, candidates are given the first line of a two-line conversation. They have to choose the appropriate response from three multiple-choice options.

PREPARATION

- Tell students to read the instructions and the example. They should read each multiple-choice answer carefully and decide which is the right response.
- A knowledge of grammar can often help students to choose the right answer. Exercise 3 focuses on questions and tenses.
- It is a good idea for students to think of an appropriate response **before** they read the multiple-choice options. Exercise 4 encourages students to think of their own response.
- Before students do the exam task, you could tell them to close their books. Then read out the questions and elicit possible responses.
- Remind them to use the clues given to help them with the task.

PREPARATION   Part 3 Key

Exercise 1

1 Five conversations.   2 On the answer sheet.

Exercise 2

1 'Where do you come from?'
2 Options **B** and **C** are not towns or countries.

Exercise 3

a⟩ 1 When, 2 Where, 3 What, 4 Who, 5 Why, 6 How many
b⟩ 1 f), 2 a), 3 e), 4 b), 5 c), 6 d)

Exercise 4
Possible answers:
1 Yes, I do. / No, I don't.
2 Yes, I am. / No, I'm not.
3 I'm fine, thanks. / I'm not feeling very well.
4 Yes, please! / No, thanks.
5 I'm not sure. / At six o'clock.
6 Yes, please. / No, thanks.

EXAM PRACTICE   Part 3 Key

11 B, **12** C, **13** B, **14** A, **15** A

Part 3, Questions 16–20

Teacher's notes

Questions 16–20 are matching questions. Candidates have to complete a longer dialogue by choosing from a list of options. There are two extra options which candidates do not need to use. The conversation may take place in a hotel, restaurant, school, café, shop, etc.

PREPARATION

- Point out that the instructions always give information about the type of conversation. The example shows how the conversation begins. This helps students predict the content.

- Reading the line after the gap as well as the one before will help them to choose the best response from the options. Exercise 3 provides practice in this strategy.
- Encourage students to read the whole conversation first so they understand the context.
- They should read it again when they finish in order to check their answers.
- Have students act out the conversation in the exam practice. They can then role-play the conversations in Exercise 6 orally.

PREPARATION   Part 3 Key

Exercise 1

1 A shop assistant and customer in a shop which sells CD players.
2 On the answer sheet.

Exercise 2

1 'Can I help you?'
2 'Yes, please.' We can then explain what help we need.
3 The customer bought a CD player but there's something wrong with it.

Exercise 3

a⟩ I need some information for a sports project.
b⟩ Yes, but I have to go to class now. Can I take it home?

Exercise 4

1 'When did you buy it?'
2 'Well, I can give you your money back or change the CD player for a new one.'
3 The customer decides to ask for his/her money back. In the next line, the assistant says: 'Certainly'. Can you write your name on this form for me, please?' Then: 'Here's your money, eighty-nine pounds fifty.'

Exercise 6
Possible answers:
Sample 1
B: Hello, can I help you?
A: Yes, I bought this pair of jeans last week and there's something wrong with them.
B: Really? What's the problem?
A: The zip is broken.
B: When did you buy the jeans?
A: On Saturday.
B: Do you have the receipt?
A: Here you are.
B: Thank you. Would you like your money back or another pair of jeans?
A: I'd like another pair of jeans, please.
Sample 2
A: Good afternoon. Do you need any help?
B: I got this bag from you yesterday and it's broken.
A: What's the matter with it?
B: Well, the handle has come off!
A: Oh dear. Can I see it please?
B: Yes, of course.
A: Well, I can change the bag or give you your money back.
B: I want my money back please – it cost twelve pounds fifty (£12.50).
A: Certainly.

Part 4, Questions 21–27

Teacher's notes

In this Part, candidates need to be able to understand the main ideas and some details in a factual text of about 180 words. The texts are adapted from an authentic source such as a magazine or newspaper. The questions may be three-option multiple-choice questions. Alternatively, candidates may be asked to decide if statements are correct or incorrect, or whether there is not enough information to decide.

PREPARATION

- For text-based tasks, candidates should always read the instructions and the title to get an idea of the topic and try to predict what they are going to read. They should then read the whole text once quickly for general understanding. Exercises 1–3 encourage students to do this.
- Exercise 4 focuses students' attention on the key parts of the text in preparation for the multiple-choice task. Check answers before students do the exam task.
- Discuss the example before telling students to do the exam task.
- Remind students to use the clues to help them with the exam task.

PREPARATION   Part 4 Key

Exercise 1
1 Seven questions.
2 The life of a supermarket manager.
3 Read and answer multiple-choice comprehension questions.
4 On the answer sheet.

Exercise 2
Answers will vary. Students will probably not predict:
emails / meetings

Exercise 3
manager, supermarket, emails, money, meetings

Exercise 4
 1 'worked in his father's mini-market'.
 2 'his present job ... with Saver Mall'
 3 '... he joined Saver Mall as a trainee manager.' 'he got his present job as a supermarket manager'
 4 He travels. 'I spend most of my time travelling by road ...'
 5 He started at 3 o'clock in the afternoon and finished at 11 p.m. 'Last week I worked from 3 p.m. to 11 p.m.'
 6 He will start at 7 in the morning and finish at 3 in the afternoon. 'from 7 a.m. to 3 p.m.'
 7 He checks his emails. 'The first thing I do each day is check my emails.'
 8 Going to different countries to check how supermarkets are doing. 'That's my favourite part of the job.'
 9 'I usually go straight to bed.'
10 Yes. 'I'm happy working for Saver Mall.'

Exercise 5
1 'went to college **and then** worked in his father's mini-market.'

2 No. The text says nothing about Jonathan working while he was at college.
3 Before.
   Therefore the answer is C.

EXAM PRACTICE   Part 4 Key

21 C; **22** C; **23** A; **24** C; **25** B; **26** C; **27** A

Part 5, Questions 28–35

Teacher's notes

In Part 5, candidates are tested on their understanding of grammar and English usage in the context of a reading text. The text is adapted from a newspaper or magazine or similar authentic source. Words are deleted from the text and candidates have to choose the appropriate words from three options. The deleted words are usually structural items such as forms of verbs, pronouns, conjunctions, determiners, prepositions, etc. Students should have a knowledge of how prepositions and other words go together at the phrase and sentence level.

PREPARATION

- Exercises 1 and 2 encourage students to read the instructions and the example carefully and to think about the grammar being tested, in this case the choice of preposition.
- Exercises 3 and 4 focus on two key grammatical areas often tested in this task, prepositions and quantifiers.
- Exercise 3 can be done orally, then students can ask and answer in pairs.
- Elicit other nouns which can follow the quantity words given in Exercise 4.
- Make sure students read the whole text before they start filling in the gaps.
- Tell them to write the words they choose in the gaps (not just the letters). This will help them to check their answers make sense when they read the text through again.

PREPARATION   Part 5 Key

Exercise 1
1 Travelling by train.   2 Eight questions.
3 On the answer sheet.

Exercise 2
1 We can say 'going **on a** train' but not 'going **on** train.' The missing word is 'a'.
2 This is not possible. 'Train' in this context is a noun, not a verb.

Exercise 3
a⟩ 1 in, 2 in, 3 by, on, 4 from, to, 5 at, 6 to

Exercise 4

a⟩

Countable		Uncountable	
some *any* *many* *few* *lots of* *no*	passengers windows	*some* *any* *much* *little* *lots of* *no*	food time

b⟩ 1 lots of, 2 some, 3 Many, 4 few, 5 any, 6 lots of

Exercise 5

Because it's exciting.

Part 6, Questions 36–40

In Part 6, candidates are tested on reading and identifying appropriate words, as well as on spelling. Candidates are given five dictionary–type sentences, plus one integrated example, and are required to identify the items from the definitions. The first letter of each word is given. Candidates should spell each word correctly.

PREPARATION

- Tell students to read the instructions and the example carefully.
- They should read the definitions and decide which word is appropriate.
- Correct spelling is important here.
- Before students do the exam task, you could tell them to close their books. Then read out the definitions and elicit possible responses.
- Remind students that each line represents one letter.

PREPARATION   Part 6 Key

Exercise 1

a⟩

Jobs	School	Travel
baker, chemist, footballer, mechanic, student waiter	whiteboard, classroom, homework, library	airport, journey, luggage, platform, ticket

b⟩ (a) Mary, (b) Ben, (c) Josie, (d) Simon, (e), (f), (g), Megan, Ian, James (in any order)

Exercise 2

1 mechanic, 2 platform, 3 grandparents, 4 chemist, 5 husband

Exercise 3

Various answers possible

Exercise 4

1 Things you can read
2 Five questions
3 On the answer sheet

Part 7, Questions 41–50

Teacher's notes

Part 7 requires candidates to complete a gapped text, usually a note or a short letter. The gaps focus on grammar and some vocabulary. Candidates are only expected to produce words which they should have active knowledge of. Correct spelling is essential.

PREPARATION

- Exercises 1–5 focus on types of words that may be deleted in the exam.
- Exercise 6 focuses on spelling.
- You can provide further sentence-level practice for this part by 'gapping out' words from sentences in things students have written, or from short texts in books.
- Exercises 7 and 8 encourage students to read the instructions and the whole text **before** they start filling in the gaps.
- Remind students to use the clues to help them with the task. These encourage them to think about what kind of word or part of speech is needed in the gaps.
- Tell them to write their choices in the gaps and to read the whole text again when they have finished to check it makes sense.

PREPARATION   Part 7 Key

Exercise 1

a⟩ 1 verb, 2 noun, 3 adjective, 4 verb, 5 noun
b⟩ 1 speak, 2 room, 3 strange, 4 get, 5 teacher

Exercise 2

a⟩ 1 walk, 2 is playing, 3 went, 4 were doing, 5 arrived, 6 have been, 7 haven't bought, 8 am going, 9 will bring, 10 am going
b⟩ 1 going, 2 is, 3 will, 4 did, 5 am

Exercise 3

1 B, 2 A, 3 C, 4 C, 5 C

Exercise 4

1 a, 2 a, 3 the, 4 I, 5 the / a, 6 we, 7 a, 8 the, 9 a, 10 it

Exercise 5

1 but, 2 and, 3 because, 4 so, 5 or

Exercise 6

41 for, 42 your, 43 great, 44 There, 45 coming, 46 which, 47 too, 48 before, 49 know, 50 with

Exercise 7

1 A note.   2 Ten questions.   3 On the answer sheet.

Exercise 8

1 From Melina.   2 To Christina.   3 A school trip.

Part 8, Questions 51–55

Teacher's notes

In Part 8, candidates have to read and write down appropriate words or numbers. This is a simple information transfer task. The test focus here is on content and accuracy. There are one or two short input texts, usually a note or an advert, or some other authentic-type text. The text prompts candidates to complete a form or a notice. There are five spaces to complete with one or more words or numbers, plus an integrated example.

PREPARATION

- Exercises 1–3 focus on useful vocabulary for forms.
- Students need to be familiar with different forms of dates and to be able to change verbs into nouns, e.g., *She teaches* > *She's **a teacher***.
- Elicit more countries for the table in Exercise 1 and tell students to write the nationalities and languages.
- You can provide further practice for Part 8 by 'gapping out' words from things that students have written, or from short texts in books.
- Exercises 4 and 5 focus on the correct way to fill out a form. Encourage students always to check their spelling and use of capital letters.
- Remind students to use the clues to help them complete the form.

PREPARATION   Part 8 Key

Exercise 1

Nationality	Language
French	French
German	German
Italian	Italian
Mexican	Spanish
Russian	Russian
Spanish	Spanish
American	English
British	English
Japanese	Japanese

Exercise 2

a⟩ 1 The thirteenth of July, nineteen ninety-one.
    2 The thirtieth of September, nineteen eighty-five.
    3 The first of April, nineteen seventy-seven.
    4 The eighteenth of December, twenty-ten / two thousand and ten.

b⟩ 1 13 July 1991 or 13/7/91
    2 30 September 1985 or 30/09/85
    3 1 April 1977 or 1/4/77
    4 18 December 2010 or 18/12/10

Exercise 3

manager, teacher, student, farmer, writer, banker

Exercise 4

1 Mr and Mrs Arnold.
2 Two students from Spain to stay with them.
3 Fill in the information on the application form.
4 Five questions.
5 On the answer sheet.

Exercise 5

51 Arnold, 52 27 River Road, Cambridge, 53 teacher,
54 20/3/71, 55 Spanish

Exercise 6

1 David.   2 A job application form.

EXAM PRACTICE   Part 8 Key

51 Cassidy, **52** 16 / sixteen, **53** American,
54 31/08 or 31 August, **55** French

Part 9, Question 56

Teacher's notes

In Part 9, candidates write a short note, message or postcard (about 25–35 words). There is either a short input text or instructions to prompt the candidates to respond. There are always three items of information to communicate. Candidates are not penalised for writing more than 25 words, though they are not advised to do this. See the mark scheme for Part 9 on page 3 of the Teacher's Book.

PREPARATION

- Students should always read the instructions carefully and identify the information they must include in their answer.
- In Exercise 2, students compare three sample answers for content and accuracy. Encourage them to check back to the task to find which samples contain all the necessary information.
- Candidates are expected to begin the note or message with the correct greeting and end it by signing their name.
- Encourage students always to check spelling and punctuation carefully when they have finished.

PREPARATION   Part 9 Key

Exercise 1

1 A notice.
2 Three questions: **where** you lost your Discman, **what** it **looks like**, **how** to return it.
3 20–25 words
4 On the back of the answer sheet.

Exercise 2

1 A, 2 C, 3 B

Exercise 3

A 1 have lost, 2 It, 3 find
B 1 classroom, 2 Saturday, 3 white, 4 to, 5 break, 6 Wednesday, 7 Thank
C 1 lost, 2 office, 3 ago, 4 There, 5 find, 6 in, 7 'the' is not needed

Exercise 4

1 A note.
2 Three questions: **what** you lost, **when** and **where** you lost it, you want to replace it
3 My friend (NAME) X

EXAM PRACTICE   Part 9 Key

Sample answer (28 words)

Hi (NAME)!
I'm very sorry! I left your book on the bus yesterday. I was going to school. Please let me buy you a new one.
Bye,
Jonathan.

Test 1

Paper 2 Listening

The Listening Paper is divided into five parts, with 25 questions. Each listening text is heard twice. There are pauses for candidates to look at the questions and to write their answers. Candidates write their answers on the question paper as they listen. They are then given eight minutes at the end of the test to transfer their answers to the answer sheet.

Note: Many of the Preparation exercises for Test 1 Paper 2 involve listening to the cassette.

Part 1, Questions 1–5

Teacher's Notes

In Part 1, candidates are tested on their ability to identify simple, factual information in five separate conversations. The conversations may be between friends or relatives, a shop assistant and a customer, a waiter and a restaurant guest, etc. The factual information is e.g. numbers, prices, times, dates, locations, shapes, sizes, the weather, descriptions of people and places, etc.

On the question paper, candidates see a question and three multiple-choice options based on pictures or drawings. Each conversation is heard twice.

PREPARATION

- Exercises 1 and 2 give students practice in discriminating between similar sounding numbers.
- Exercise 3 practises the different ways of telling the time.
- Exercise 4 practises shapes. Ask students to think of more everyday objects which are square, round or rectangular.
- Exercises 6 and 7 help to familiarise students with the format of the task. Play the recording. Point out that the questions are on the recording as well as on the exam paper.

PREPARATION Part 1 Key

Exercise 1
1 a), 2 b), 3 b), 4 a), 5 a), 6 b), 7 a)

Exercise 2
a) 2 £16.95 (sixteen pounds, ninety-five pence),
3 30p (thirty pence),
4 £60.13 (sixty pounds, thirteen),
5 £50.25 (fifty pounds, twenty-five)
b) 1 £49.99 (forty-nine pounds, ninety-nine),
2 £130 (one hundred and thirty pounds),
3 50p (fifty pence),
4 £7.25 (seven pounds and twenty-five pence,
5 £13.70 (thirteen pounds, seventy)

Exercise 3
a) 1 half past three, 2 ten past six, 3 quarter to eight,
4 two o'clock
b) 1 It's three thirty, 2 It's six ten, 3 It's seven forty-five
c) 1 a, 2 b, 3 a, 4 b, 5 a

Exercise 4
a) 1 square, 2 circle, 3 triangle, 4 rectangle
b) 1 round / circular, 2 rectangular, 3/4 Answers will vary.

Exercise 5
1 Five conversations.
2 Three pictures.
3 Twice / Two times.
4 You put a tick under the right answer.

Exercise 6
1 What time is it?   2 Five o'clock.
3 There is a tick in box B.

PREPARATION Part 1 Tapescripts

Exercise 1 Numbers
1 Thirteen   5 Forty
2 Ninety   6 Eighty
3 Fifteen   7 Twenty-five
4 Seventeen

Exercise 2b Prices
1 **Woman:** Excuse me, how much are these jeans, please?
Shop assistant: They're forty-nine ninety-nine.
Woman: Forty-nine ninety-nine? Can I try them on?

2 **Boy:** Could you tell me the price of this CD player?
Shop assistant: That one's a hundred and thirty pounds.
Boy: A hundred and thirty pounds. That's very expensive.

3 **Girl:** Are those apples fifty pence a kilo?
Shop assistant: Yes, that's right, fifty p.

4 **Cinema-goer:** Can I have one ticket for Star Wars, please?
Assistant: Seven pounds twenty-five, please.
Cinema-goer: Sorry?
Assistant: Seven pounds twenty-five.

5 **Mother:** I like your shoes. How much did you pay for them?
Girl: Only thirteen pounds seventy.
Mother: Thirteen pounds seventy? That's cheap.

Exercise 3c Telling the time
1 **Man:** When does the library open, please?
Woman: At nine fifteen.
Man: Nine fifteen. Thanks.

2 **Boy:** What time is it now?
Girl: It's twenty-five to ten. Why?
Boy: There's a good film on at ten.
Girl: Oh, in twenty-five minutes.

3 **Son:** What time does the match start, Dad?
Father: It's on at three thirty.
Son: Oh, it's nearly three thirty now.

4 **Man:** When did you get here?
Woman: We arrived at quarter past twelve.
Man: Quarter past twelve? So it took you two hours to get here.

5 **Traveller:** Can you tell me what time the train leaves?
Conductor: At eight thirty-five.
Traveller: Eight thirty-five. Thanks.

1 A, **2** A, **3** C, **4** B, **5** B

EXAM PRACTICE   Part 1 Tapescript

Look at the instructions for Part One. You will hear five short conversations. You will hear each conversation twice. There is one question for each conversation. For questions 1–5, put a tick under the right answer. Here is an example:

What time is it?
Woman: Excuse me, can you tell me what time it is?
Man: Yes, it's <u>five o'clock</u>.
Woman: Thanks.
Man: That's all right.

The answer is five o'clock, so there is a tick in box B. Now we are ready to start. Look at question one.

1 *How much did John's football shirt cost?*
Girl: That's a great football shirt, John – was it expensive?
Boy: Not really. <u>Thirteen pounds twenty-five.</u>
Girl: That's quite cheap!
Boy: Yes, it is.
Now listen again.
[REPEAT]

2 *Which cake does the woman want?*
Baker: Good morning madam. Can I help you?
Shopper: Yes, I'd like that cake. <u>The white one.</u>
Baker: Do you want the square one or the round one?
Shopper: Oh, I don't mind – but I think I'll take <u>the round one</u>.
Now listen again.

3 *What size shoe does the man take?*
Shop assistant: Would you like to try those shoes on, sir?
Shopper: Yes, but they're size eight and too small for me.
Shop assistant: What size are you, sir?
Shopper: <u>I'm a size nine.</u>
Now listen again.

4 *When is Anna's birthday?*
Man: It's Anna's birthday soon, isn't it?
Woman: Yes, it is. Mine is the thirteenth of September and hers is a couple of weeks later.
Man: <u>On the thirtieth</u>, right?
Woman: Yes.
Now listen again.

5 *What is Petros going to buy?*
Girl: Hi, Petros. What are you doing here?
Boy: I'm trying to think of something to buy Christine for her birthday.
Girl: Well, I've bought her a book and Paulo's got her a T-shirt. <u>Why don't you buy her a CD?</u>
Boy: <u>That's a good idea – I think I will.</u>
Now listen again.

This is the end of Part One.

Part 2, Questions 6–10

Teacher's Notes

In Part 2, candidates identify simple, factual information in a longer conversation. The conversation is an informal one, usually between two people who know each other. The topic is often about daily life, free time activities, hobbies, school,

travel, etc. Candidates have to match two lists of items. There are always two extra options which are not needed. The conversation is heard twice.

PREPARATION

- Use Exercise 1 to familiarise students with the exam task.
- Exercise 2 revises the vocabulary of free time activities.
- Exercise 3 revises useful weather vocabulary. (**Note:** this vocabulary is tested in Test 1, Paper 3, Speaking and Test 2, Paper 2 Part 1. See Students' Book pages 43 and 67.)
- Tell students to read through the list of options before you play the recording.
- Tell them to answer as many questions as they can during the first listening, but not to worry if they miss a question.
- Let students compare their answers before playing the recording again. Tell them to check and complete their answers.

PREPARATION   Part 2 Key

Exercise 1
1 Five questions.
2 Paul and Jane.
3 Paul's holiday in Scotland.
4 Days and Activities.
5 Eight activities (three more than the number of questions).
6 Twice.
7 By writing the correct letter in the box.

Exercise 2
a〉 **Possible answers**
2 In picture 2 they are watching a pop concert / listening to rock music.
3 In picture 3, two friends are talking together in a café.
4 In picture 4, they are playing basketball.
5 In picture 5, the girl is reading a book.
6 In picture 6, the girls are shopping.
7 In picture 7, they are bowling / at a bowling alley.

c〉 **Possible questions**
2 How often do you go to pop concerts?
3 How often do you go to the café with your friends?
4 How often do you play basketball?
5 How often do you read books?
6 How often do you go shopping?
7 How often do you go bowling?

Exercise 3
a〉 🎧 1 b, 2 c, 3 a

PREPARATION   Part 2 Tapescript

Exercise 3〉 The weather
Boy: Hi! Did you have a good time last weekend?
Girl: Yes, great thanks.
Boy: What was the weather like?
Girl: Well, on <u>Saturday morning</u> when we arrived, it was terrible! It was very <u>cold and windy</u>.
Boy: Oh, no! How terrible!
Girl: Yes, and then <u>in the afternoon it rained</u>.
Boy: What about <u>on Sunday</u> – did the weather get better?
Girl: Yes, it was <u>hot and sunny</u> in the morning so we went to the beach.
Boy: Oh, that was lucky.

6 C, **7** B, **8** D, **9** H, **10** G

Listen to Paul talking to Jane about his holiday in Scotland. What did he do on each day? For questions 6–10, write a letter A–H next to each day. You will hear the conversation twice.

Jane: Hi, Paul, tell me about your holiday in Scotland!

Paul: Well, I arrived on Friday evening and on Saturday I <u>did some shopping</u>. I bought a pair of trousers. Then on Sunday I went to the Rock and Roll <u>museum</u>.

Jane: Do they have Michael Jackson there?

Paul: Well, a model of him, yes! Then on Monday I wanted to go swimming, but it was too cold, so I <u>played football</u>. That was great!

Jane: And on Tuesday? What did you do?

Paul: Well, Tuesday was a long day because <u>I went on a day trip to Edinburgh</u>. I went sightseeing and I saw lots of famous places.

Jane: Wow, did you see the castle?

Paul: Yes! Then on Wednesday I didn't go anywhere 'cos I was too tired. I just <u>played computer games</u> and wrote some postcards to my family.

Jane: And on Thursday?

Paul: It was a beautiful sunny day, so I <u>went swimming</u>. Then on Friday I had to leave! What did you do for your holiday, Jane?

Jane: I studied for my exams!

Paul: Oh!

Now listen again.

This is the end of Part Two.

Part 3, Questions 11–15

Teacher's Notes

In Part 3, candidates also identify simple, factual information in a longer conversation. The conversation is usually an informal one between two people who know each other. It may be a transactional exchange of some type, e.g. a person making enquiries at a travel agent's, etc. There are five questions with three-option multiple-choice answers. Candidates have to tick the correct answer.

- Encourage students to read the instructions carefully, using Exercise 1.
- The questions in this Part may focus on measurements and describing objects. Exercises 2 and 3 revise useful vocabulary.
- In Exercise 3a⟩, elicit more words to add to the table.
- You could give students further practice by describing everyday objects to them. Include measurements and the shape. Students have to guess what the objects are.
- For the exam task, encourage students to answer as many questions as they can during the first listening, but not to worry if they miss a question.
- Let students compare their answers before playing the recording again. Tell them to check and complete their answers.

Exercise 1

1 John is phoning a shop.
2 John wants to buy something.
3 You tick the correct answer.
4 Twice.

Exercise 2

a⟩ ⌒
    1 fifteen metres (15m),
    2 fifty centimetres (50cm),
    3 one metre ninety (1m 90cm),
    4 nine metres twenty (9m 20cm),
    5 five metres ninety-five (5m 95cm)

b⟩ 1 3m 75cm, 2 80cm, 3 1m 25cm, 4 2m 5cm, 5 3m 30cm

Exercise 3

a⟩

Size	Materials	Objects
long, wide, short, high, tall, deep,	wood, wool, plastic, nylon, leather, cotton	jacket, wardrobe, scarf, belt, pencil case, watch

b⟩ 1 long, 2 tall, 3 high, 4 long, 5 high
c⟩ ⌒ 2 1m 89, 3 2m 20, 4 40cm, 5 1m 7

Exercise 2a⟩ Measurements

1 fifteen metres	4 nine metres twenty
2 fifty centimetres	5 five metres ninety-five
3 one metre ninety	

Exercise 3c⟩ Describing things

1 Man: Excuse me, how long is that table?
  Woman: The one in the corner? It's <u>one metre seventy-five</u> long. Six people can sit there.

2 Girl: How tall is Nick? He's taller than Christo, isn't he?
  Boy: Yes, Nick is <u>one metre eighty-nine</u>.

3 Woman: Will the wardrobe go through the door? How high is it?
  Man: Let's measure it. Oh, dear, it's <u>two metres twenty</u>.

4 Woman: I like that skirt. Could you tell me how long it is, please?
  Shop assistant: It's <u>forty centimetres</u>.
  Woman: Oh, quite short!

5 Son: How high is a tennis net?
  Father: It's ninety-one centimetres in the middle but at the ends it's <u>one metre seven</u>.

11 B, **12** C, **13** A, **14** B, **15** A

Listen to John phoning a shop about something he wants to buy. For Questions 11–15, tick A, B or C. You will hear the conversation twice.

Assistant: Good morning, Camping Bags and Tents, <u>Oxford Street</u>. How can I help you?

John: Oh, good morning. I'd like some information, please. I saw some <u>rucksacks</u> in your shop window yesterday.

Assistant: Oh, yes, we have several different kinds. Our best-selling rucksack is the Weekender.

John: How big is it?

Assistant: It's forty centimetres by sixty centimetres.

John: Oh, I think that's too small. I need it when I go camping next weekend.

Assistant: Well, we also have the Weekender Plus. That's seventy by ninety, no, sorry, <u>sixty by ninety</u>.

John: That's better. What's it made of? I don't want plastic or canvas.

Assistant: All our rucksacks are made of <u>nylon</u>.

John: Great. What colours do you have?

Assistant: The Plus is available in red and green, or blue and white.

John: Can you keep <u>a blue and white one</u> for me, please? I'll come and get it on Saturday.

Assistant: Certainly, sir. The price is usually thirty-nine, ninety-five, but it's on sale now at only twenty-nine, ninety-five.

John: That's fine. Thank you very much for your help.

This is the end of Part 3.

Parts 4 and 5, Questions 16–25

Teacher's Notes

In Part 4, candidates listen to a dialogue, which usually takes place in a shop or an office. In Part 5, candidates listen to a monologue which is usually a recorded message. In both Parts 4 and 5, candidates have to extract specific information, such as opening times, prices, entrance fees, etc. and complete a set of notes, a message or a memo. Candidates only have to write one or two words or a number for each question. Completely accurate spelling is not required, except if a name has been spelled out on the recording, or the word is a simple, high frequency one. Both Parts 4 and 5 are heard twice.

- Encourage students to read the instructions carefully, using Exercise 1.
- Students need plenty of practice in predicting the **type** of answer that is needed, as in Exercise 2.
- Tell students to complete as many answers as they can during the first listening, but not to worry if they miss a question.
- They can check and complete their answers on the second listening.
- Encourage students to check they have not written more than two words per answer and that their spelling is correct.
- The communication activity in Exercise 6 focuses on useful functional language which may be needed in the exam. Check answers to the gapped dialogue before students do the role play.

Exercise 1
1 Five questions.   2 A tourist guide.
3 Places to have lunch.   4 On the form.
5 Twice.

Exercise 2
16 c, 17 e, 18 d, 19 a, 20 b

16 three / 3, **17** bus station, **18** six / 6, **19** Blue Sky, **20** fish

You will hear a tourist guide talking to some tourists about places to have lunch in Bournemouth. Listen and complete questions 16–20. You will hear the conversation twice.

Tour guide: Listen everybody, please. You're now <u>free to do what you want until three o'clock</u> this afternoon, when we will visit Bournemouth Zoo.

Tourist: Where can we get something to eat?

Tour guide: There are lots of places to eat in Bournemouth. There are pizzerias and fast food restaurants near the <u>bus station</u>, but why not try one of the seafood cafés near the beach?

Tourist: Do the meals cost a lot there?

Tour guide: No, you can eat for about <u>six pounds</u> and the meals are large.

Tourist: What other places are good for lunch?

Tour guide: Well, there's a hotel not far from the bus station. It's called the <u>Blue Sky Hotel</u> – you can get an excellent three-course lunch for only eight pounds and ninety five pence.

Tourist: What time does the hotel restaurant open?

Tour guide: It's open between twelve thirty and half past three.

Tourist: I don't want to go to a restaurant. I want to go shopping!

Tour guide: Why not buy some <u>fish</u> and chips? They only cost about two pounds fifty and you can eat them as you walk along the street! Enjoy your lunch everyone and remember to be back here at three o'clock.

Now listen again.

This is the end of Part Four.

Exercise 6
a⟩ a / Can I have / for / some / anything / I'd like
b⟩ 🎧 **Tapescript**
See Students' Book page 36 and Answer Key above.

Teacher's Notes

- Exercises 1 and 2 give students practice in reading the instructions to the exam task and predicting the **type** of information that is missing in the notes.
- Exercise 3 revises phone numbers, which are often tested in the exam.

Exercise 1
1 Five questions.
2 Some information about a museum.
3 On the form.
4 Twice.

Exercise 2
21 c) a time, 22 d) a price, 23 e) a kind of visitor,
24 a) something to eat, 25 b) a phone number

Exercise 3
a)
   1 020 85 21 79 66 (oh two oh, eight five, two one, seven
     nine, double six)
   2 07 837 52 69 40 (oh seven, eight three seven, five two,
     six nine, four oh)
   3 01962 85 57 63 (oh one nine six two, eight five, five
     seven, six three)
   4 01223 55 88 22 (oh one double two three, double five,
     double eight, double two)
   5 01736 740 169 (oh one seven three six, seven four oh,
     one six nine)

Exercise 3〉 Telephone numbers
1 **Girl 1:** What's Maria's new phone number?
  Boy: Sorry, I don't know.
  Girl 2: It's <u>oh two oh, eight five, two one, seven nine,
  double six</u>.
  Girl 1: 020 85 21 79 66. Thanks.

2 **Boy:** Can you remember Christos' mobile number?
  Girl: Yes, it's <u>oh seven, eight three seven, five two, six
  nine, four oh</u>.
  Boy: OK, I'll give him a ring now. 0-7-8-3-7 5-2 6-9
  4-0.

3 **Girl:** John, have you got the number for the Mega
  Screen Cinema?
  Boy: Wait a minute. Let me look in the phone book.
  Here it is – <u>oh one nine six two, eight five, five seven,
  six three</u>.
  Girl: 01962 ...?
  Boy: 85 57 63.
  Girl: Thanks.

4 **Man:** Hello, is that oh one double two three, <u>double
  five, double eight, double two</u>?
  Woman: No, this is 01223 88 55 22.
  Man: Sorry, wrong number. I wanted 55 88 22.

5 **Woman:** Hello, Directory Enquiries, which town,
  please?
  Boy: Can you tell me the number of the Football
  News Service, please?
  Voice: The number you require is <u>oh one seven three
  six, seven four oh, one six nine</u>. I repeat: 01736 740 169.

21 6.30 p.m. / six thirty in the evening,
22 £2.50 / two pounds and fifty pence, **23** families,
24 hot food, **25** 85 57 37 (eight five, five seven, three seven)

*You will hear some information about a museum. Listen and
complete questions 21–25. You will hear the conversation
twice.*

Thank you for calling the Winchester Museum. This is a
recorded message. The museum is open every day except
Sundays from nine o'clock in the morning <u>to six thirty in the
evening</u>. The latest time you can enter the museum is five
o'clock. On Sundays the museum opens at ten, closes at
four and the latest entry time is two thirty. Tickets cost four
pounds forty for adults and <u>two pounds fifty for children</u>.
Students pay three pounds if they have their student card. If
you are over sixty-five, you pay the same as students but
you must bring your ID card with you. There are <u>special
prices for</u> large groups and <u>families</u>. There is a café, which is
open every day from ten o'clock to four o'clock and <u>serves
hot food</u> and snacks. Please phone during office hours nine
o'clock to five thirty for more information. The telephone
number is Winchester <u>eight five, five seven, three seven</u>.
Thank you for calling the Winchester museum.
Now listen again.

This is the end of Part Five.

Test 1

Paper 3   Speaking

Part 1

Teacher's Notes

Part 1 takes 5–6 minutes. There are two examiners: one who
speaks to the candidates (the interlocutor) and one who
assesses their spoken English (the assessor). The   candidate speaks with the interlocutor, answering factual questions about their name, place of study (or work),
hobbies, daily habits, etc. The interlocutor will alternate
between the two candidates. Candidates do not have to talk
to their partner in this part of the test.

Students should learn how to talk about themselves, where
they come from, etc. They should also be ready to spell their
name and address.

• Exercises 1–2 give students guided practice in asking and
  answering questions of the type they may be asked in the
  exam, including spelling.
• For the exam task, the questions are on the tape. Put
  students into pairs, A and B. Play the questions for
  Student A, pausing after each question. Student A should
  address his/her answers to Student B.
• Then do the same for Student B's questions. This way, the
  whole class can practise simultaneously.

Exercise 1
a) A /eɪ/   C /sɪː/   E /ɪː/   G /dʒiː/   H /eitʃ/   I /aɪ/
   J /dʒeɪ/   K /keɪ/   N /cn/   Q /kjuː/   U /juː/   V /viː/
   W /ˈdʌbəljuː/   X /eks/   Y /waɪ/   Z /zed/

b) double + name of letter e.g. double *e*
c) 🎧 QUIGLEY / FARRINGDON / LATIMER

Exercise 2 🎧
1 d, 2 c, 3 e, 4 a, 5 f, 6 b

PREPARATION   Part 1 Tapescripts

Exercise 1c) Spelling
Woman: Hello, I'm Susan Summers. What's your name, please?
Boy: Jason Quigley.
Woman: Could you spell your surname for me, please, Jason?
Boy: Yes, it's Q-U-I-G-L-E-Y.
Woman: Thank you. And what town do you come from?
Boy: I live in Farringdon, F-A- double R-I-N-G-D-O-N.
Woman: And what's your address?
Boy: It's twenty-five, Latimer Street.
Woman: How do you spell that, please?
Boy: L-A-T-I-M-E-R Street.
Woman: Thank you. Now I'd like to …

Exercise 2b) Giving personal information
Man: What's the name of your school?
Girl: Woodgrange Secondary School. It's near my home.
Man: Do you like going to school?
Girl: Yes, I do. I have lots of friends there.
Man: What is your favourite subject at school?
Girl: Geography. It's very interesting.
Man: Do you have any brothers and sisters?
Girl: Yes, I have one brother and one sister.
Man: What sort of music do you like?
Girl: I like all pop music.
Man: What do you usually do at weekends?
Girl: I usually visit my friends and sometimes I go to the cinema.

EXAM PRACTICE   Part 1 Key

Answers will vary.

EXAM PRACTICE   Part 1 Tapescript

You will hear an examiner asking some questions.
Student A, listen carefully and answer the questions.

What's your name?
Can you spell your surname for me, please?
What school do you go to?
Which subjects do you like best?
What do you do at the weekends?
Thank you.

You will hear an examiner asking some questions.
Student B, listen carefully and answer the questions.

What's your name?
What's your address?
Can you spell the name of your street, please?
Do you have any brothers and sisters?
What kind of music do you like?
Thank you.

Part 2

Teacher's Notes

Part 2 takes 3–4 minutes. The two candidates interact with each other, taking turns to ask and answer questions. Prompt cards are used to cue the questions and answers. These will be related to leisure activities, hobbies and sports, daily life, etc. Candidates have to ask (or answer) five questions. Then their roles are reversed.

The prompt cards stimulate questions of a non-personal kind, in this case about a snack bar, a magazine and a competition.

A variety of questions will be acceptable. Candidate B is expected to give appropriate answers to the questions asked, with reference to his/her personal experience or his/her role card.

PREPARATION

- Exercises 1 and 2 familiarise students with what they have to do and give them practice in constructing accurate and appropriate questions and answers.
- After checking the questions in Exercises 1b) and 2b), elicit possible answers based on the picture prompts.
- Before the pairwork practice, point out that there may be other acceptable ways to make questions from the prompts. Elicit other possible questions.
- For the exam practice, elicit possible questions from the prompts before letting students work in pairs. Give them a time limit of two to three minutes to ask and answer questions based on each prompt card, to give them an idea of exam conditions.

PREPARATION   Part 2 Key

Exercise 1
a) 1 Information about a snack bar.
   2 No.
   3 B has to ask A's questions about the snack bar.
   4 There is no need to write anything.

Exercise 2
1 When does the snack bar open?
2 What fruit juices can you buy?
3 What is the special food?
4 What is the address?
5 What is the telephone number?

EXAM PRACTICE   Part 2 Key

MAGAZINE - possible questions and answers.

What is the name of the magazine?	Music Lovers' Magazine
How much does it cost?	three pounds
Who is it for?	children
What type of music?	classical
Is anything free?	free CD

COMPETITION - possible questions and answers.

Is it for adults?	No, for children
What do you have to draw?	your favourite animal
When is the last day?	2 May
What do you win?	a trip to the zoo
What is the competition address?	46 North Road, London

Test 2

Paper 1 Reading and Writing

Part 1, Questions 1–5

Teacher's Notes

PREPARATION

- Point out that the verbs *should/shouldn't* may be used in explanations of signs. Ask students to think of things they should/shouldn't do in various places: hospital, library, supermarket, cinema, swimming pool, etc. Then tell them to do Exercise 3.
- Exercise 4 focuses on useful vocabulary for this Part.
- Remind students to use the clues to help them with the exam task.

PREPARATION Part 1 Key

Exercise 1
1 'Which notice says this?'   2 Five questions.
3 On the answer sheet.

Exercise 2
rubbish

Exercise 3
1 should, 2 should, shouldn't, 3 shouldn't , 4 should,
5 should

Exercise 4
 1 On a food packet.
 2 At the sports centre.
 3 At the theatre. ('show' would not be used in a cinema)
 4 At the shoe shop.
 5 In a museum.
 6 Outside a restaurant.
 7 In the supermarket.
 8 At the beach.
 9 In the cinema.
10 At the airport (where you check in your luggage).

EXAM PRACTICE Part 1 Key

1 B, **2** G, **3** A, **4** D, **5** C

PREPARATION

Part 2, Questions 6–10

- Exercises 3 and 4 focus on vocabulary and irregular past tense verbs. These are often tested in this part of the exam.
- Ask students to make a list of which words in English they confuse. Think about 'false friends'.
- For further practice, put students into groups for 'past tense tennis'! In turn, each group 'serves' an infinitive verb to another group; the 'receiving' group then 'returns' the verb in the past tense; the first group then 'returns' the verb in the past participle.

PREPARATION Part 2 Key

Exercise 1
1 Going shopping, 2 Five questions, 3 On the answer sheet

Exercise 2
We say *go shopping*, not ~~make shopping~~. We say *spend money*.

Exercise 3
a⟩ **go:** swimming, shopping, on holiday
   play: football, a game, the piano
   make: a noise, friends, a cake
   do: the washing up, a crossword, my homework
   spend: the day, money, time
   have: a biscuit, a party, the flu
b⟩ I went, 2 does, 3 had, 4 spends, 5 made, 6 play

Exercise 4
1 beach café, 2 bus stop, 3 CD player, 4 railway station,
5 school holiday, 6 shopping centre, 7 baseball cap

EXAM PRACTICE Part 2 Key

6 decided, **7** clothes, **8** favourite, **9** cap, **10** Later

Part 3, Questions 11–15

Teacher's notes

PREPARATION

- Explain that it will help students to choose the appropriate response if they try to understand the situation and the purpose or function of the speaker's question or statement. Exercise 3 gives them practice in doing this.
- The clues to the exam task focus on the function of the first statement and this should help students to choose the right option.
- Encourage students to check their choice by reading both lines of the exchange together.

PREPARATION Part 3 Key

Exercise 1
1 Five conversations.   2 On the answer sheet.

Exercise 2
1 b)
2 When somebody thanks you for doing something.
3 When somebody asks if they can do something.

Exercise 3
a⟩ Possible answers:
1 parent to child / the child looks unwell or is coughing
2 teacher to student / the student has passed an exam, etc.
3 student to another student / the teacher has given them a lot of homework
4 friends / it is the weekend
5 customer to shop assistant / the customer has brought the item back to the shop
b⟩ a) 5, b) 1, c) 4, e) 2, f) 3   [d) and g) are not needed]
c⟩ 1c), 2e), 3d), 4a), 5b)

EXAM PRACTICE Part 3 Key

11 C, **12** A, **13** B, **14** C, **15** A

Part 3, Questions 16–20

Teacher's notes

PREPARATION

- Remind students that they should
  - read the instructions and the example carefully to understand the context of the conversation.
  - read the line after each gap to check their choices make sense.
- Exercise 3 shows students how to approach this type of task, by reading the whole conversation first and thinking about possible responses before choosing their answers.

PREPARATION   Part 3 Key

Exercise 1
1 On the telephone.   2 Mary and Peter.
3 On the answer sheet.

Exercise 2
1 'Hello, this is (NAME).'   2 'Hi, Peter. …'

Exercise 3
a ⟩ 1 He invites her to come to a concert. She doesn't agree immediately.
2 Friends of Mario and Gina.
3 Because Gina asks about him.
4 To buy her a ticket.
5 How much they cost.
6 Four tickets.
7 Yes.
b ⟩ 1 e), 2 a), 3 f), 4 c), 5 d), 6 b)

EXAM PRACTICE   Part 3 Key

16 B, **17** H, **18** A, **19** D, **20** F

Part 4, Questions 21–27

Teacher's notes

PREPARATION

- Remind students to read the instructions and the title of the text to get an idea of the topic and try to predict what they are going to read.
- They should then read the whole text once quickly for general understanding.
- The questions in Exercise 4 encourage students to read the text again carefully for detail.
- Discuss the example before telling students to do the exam task.
- Remind students to use the clues to help them with the task.

PREPARATION   Part 4 Key

Exercise 1
1 A young boy who wants to be a football player/footballer.
2 Decide if statements are 'Right' or 'Wrong' according to the text, or if the text 'Doesn't say' i.e. there is not enough information in the text to decide.
3 On the answer sheet.

Exercise 2
Answers will vary. Students will probably predict: *goal, club, football boots, team, game*

Exercise 3
homework, goal, club, team, school

Exercise 4
1 'Jamie Zvenison, the newest and youngest football player'
2 'Jamie … was the winner!'
3 'Jamie is only … sixteen'
4 'he has always dreamed of playing football for a famous club.'
5 'He has played football all his life'
6 'when he was only six years old!'
7 'Jamie has to spend a lot of time with …'
8 'he continues his lessons with a teacher at his home'
9 'his friends … often come to watch him play football … at weekends.'

Exercise 5
1 He's sixteen.
2 Because the text says 'He's the youngest'.

EXAM PRACTICE   Part 4 Key

21 B, **22** B, **23** A, **24** A, **25** C, **26** B, **27** C

Part 5, Questions 28–35

Teacher's notes

PREPARATION

- After going through the instructions and the example, point out that comparatives and superlatives often appear in the exam and do Exercise 3.
- For further practice, you could
  - give students more adjectives, comparatives and superlatives and get them to complete a similar table to the one in Exercise 3a⟩.
  - encourage students to find out about a particular animal, and to make up similar exercises to Exercises 3b⟩ and 3c⟩ to test a partner.
- Before students do the exam task, remind them to read the whole text first for general understanding. You could check comprehension by asking: *What have you learned about sharks and whales?*
- Encourage students to write the words, not just the letters, in the gaps to help them when checking their answers. They can use the clues provided to help them with the task.

PREPARATION   Part 5 Key

Exercise 1
1 Sharks and whales.   2 Eight questions.
3 On the answer sheet.

Exercise 2
2 *Too* and *very* can't be used in this context.

Exercise 3

a

Adjective	Comparative	Superlative
long	longer	the longest
big	bigger	the biggest
dirty	dirtier	the dirtiest
dangerous	more dangerous	the most dangerous
good	better	the best
bad	worse	the worst

b 1 heavier, 2 fastest, 3 most beautiful, 4 worse, 5 better

c Possible answers:

2 The tiger is not as intelligent as the dolphin. / The dolphin is more intelligent than the tiger.

3 Whales are less dangerous than sharks / not as dangerous as sharks. / Sharks are more dangerous than whales.

4 Lions are not as fast as cheetahs. / Cheetahs are faster than lions.

5 The elephant is heavier than the rhino. / The rhino is less heavy than / not as heavy as the elephant.

EXAM PRACTICE   Part 5 Key

28 A, **29** A, **30** B, **31** C, **32** A, **33** B, **34** B, **35** A

Part 6, Questions 36–40

Teacher's notes

PREPARATION

- Exercises 3 and 4 focus on structures that are sometimes used in the descriptions of words in this Part.
- Explain the difference between *if* and *when* before students do the exercise. *If* is usually used when there is a possibility that the event might happen. *When* is usually used for general truths (an event that is a certainty).
- For further practice, ask students to write the first half of some sentences using *if* or *when*. They then give these to a partner, who has to complete the sentences.
- For further practice of *will* and *may*, ask students to make up their own predictions.

PREPARATION   Part 6 Key

Exercise 1

1 Topic: holidays.   2 Five questions.
3 On the answer sheet.

Exercise 2

Passport is the right answer because it begins with the letter P and is a travel document which has your name and photograph on it.

Exercise 3

1 c, 2 a, 3 c, 4 b, 5 f, 6 d

Exercise 4

Answers will vary.

EXAM PRACTICE   Part 6 key

36 suitcase, **37** tent, **38** camera, **39** water, **40** toothbrush

Part 7, Questions 41–50

Teacher's notes

PREPARATION

- Elicit the difference between this task and the one in Test 1: this task has **two** letters, not one.
- Verb forms are often tested in this part. Exercise 2 focuses on the choice of -*ing* or infinitive form after a main verb. Ask students to tell you what they *like / hate / don't mind / enjoy doing* and what they *hope / want / would like to do* this weekend / next summer, etc.
- Exercise 3 revises -*ing* or infinitive and some of the other grammatical points tested in Part 6.
- Check answers to Exercise 4 before students fill in the gaps in the exam task.
- Remind students to use the clues to help them with the task.
- Encourage students to write the words in the gaps to help them when checking their answers.

PREPARATION   Part 7 Key

Exercise 1

1 Two letters.
2 Ten questions.
3 On the answer sheet.

Exercise 2

1 learning, 2 to work, 3 to visit, 4 to go, 5 to come

Exercise 3

1 when, 2 to know, 3 to stay, 4 my, 5 to have, 6 studying, 7 your, 8 for, 9 it, 10 to bring, 11 to stay, 12 are

Exercise 4

1 From Matthew Martins to the Cardiff Tourist Information Office.
2 To thank them for the information they sent.
3 From Jason Brown of the Cardiff Tourist Information Office to Matthew Martins.
4 To offer further help if necessary.

EXAM PRACTICE   Part 7 Key

41 for, **42** them, **43** to, **44** am, **45** a, **46** was, **47** receive / get / read, **48** every / each, **49** their / the, **50** if

Part 8, Questions 51–55

Teacher's notes

PREPARATION

- Exercise 2 prepares students for the exam task by revising useful vocabulary for describing things. It has a similar format to Part 3, Questions 21–25.

- Tell students to read the gapped conversation all the way through without looking at the options A–H. Elicit possible responses that Darren could make.

- They then do the task and compare their ideas with the options given.
- Students can practise making up a similar dialogue, imagining they have lost one of their own possessions.
- Remind students of the correct way to fill out a form. (See Test 1 PREPARATION page 23.)
- Remind students to use the clues to help them with the task.

PREPARATION Part 8 Key

Exercise 1
1 Belinda Brown.
2 A Lost Property Form. This asks for details and a description of something that somebody has lost.

Exercise 2
a) 1 D, 2 F, 3 A, 4 H, 5 C, 6 B

EXAM PRACTICE Part 8 Key

51 (sports) bag, **52** red,
53 (5/five school) books,
54 49, **55** 8/eight

Part 9, Question 56

Teacher's notes

PREPARATION

- Students should read the note carefully and underline the questions. They should make sure that they respond to the questions in their answer.
- Exercise 2 revises vocabulary for describing people. For further practice, you could hand out pictures from magazines and ask students to write short descriptions. Put the pictures on the wall. Redistribute the descriptions to the students and get them to match the writing with the pictures.
- Exercise 3 focuses on typical errors. Remind students that they should always check their grammar and spelling when they have finished. (See the mark scheme for Part 8 on Teacher's Book page 4.)

PREPARATION Part 9 Key

Exercise 1
1 Read the note.
2 Three questions: **where** you should wait, **what** you look like, **what** clothes you will wear
3 20–25 words.

Exercise 2
a) 1 c, 2 d, 3 a, 4 b
b) Height: **tall**, **medium**, **short**   Build: **slim**, **fat**, medium
Hair: **long**, **black**, **short**, **curly**, **brown**, **bald**, **straight**, **fair**, red, dark
Face: **round**, **long**, **thin**, square, fat

Exercise 3
1 Where to wait.   2 hair / will wear / sweater / is

Exercise 4
1 A note to friend Sara.
2 Three questions: <u>What does he look like?</u>,
<u>What clothes will he wear?</u>, <u>Where will he wait for me?</u>

3 20–25 words.
4 On the back of the answer sheet.

EXAM PRACTICE Part 9 Key

Sample answer (29 words)

Dear Sara,
My brother is tall and he's got long black hair. He will wear jeans and a sweater. He will wait for you outside the bank.
Bye,
Emily.

Test 2

Paper 2   Listening

Part 1, Questions 1–5

Teacher's Notes

PREPARATION

- Exercises 1 and 2 practise the language of location and directions. You may need to play the recording for Exercise **1b** twice to let students check their answers.
- For further practice, ask students to describe where shops, etc. are in their local town and how to get there from the school.
- This Part may also require an understanding of expressions of opinion. Exercise 3 revises this language. Let students practise the three dialogues in pairs.
- Use Exercise 6 to remind students about the format of the task. Point out that the questions are on the recording as well as on the exam paper.

PREPARATION   Part 1 Key

Exercise 1
a) 1 opposite, 2 in front of, 3 on the corner of, 4 between
b) 1 Sam, 2 Lucy, 3 Paul, 4 Mandy, 5 Michael,
6 Francesca

Exercise 2
a) 1 library, 2 video shop, 3 cinema
c) **Possible answers:**
  1 A: (standing in front of the bank in Station Road)
     Can you tell me how to get to the library, please?
    B: Yes, go straight up Station Road. It's on the right, opposite the sports centre.
  2 A: (standing in front of the railway station) Can you tell me where the hotel is, please?
    B: Certainly. Go straight down Cook Street. At the crossroads turn right into High Street. You'll see the hotel at the end of the street, on your right just before the traffic lights.

Exercise 3
a) <u>I thought it was fantastic. What about you?</u>
<u>No, I don't agree. I didn't like it.</u>
<u>Who do you like best</u>, Robbie Williams or REM?

I don't like REM at all. I think their songs are terrible.
Do you think so? I like them a lot. I think they're really great.
I don't agree. I think Robbie Williams is much better. His new CD is brilliant.
Yes, he's really good.

b) **Possible answers:**
A: The murder story? What did you think of it?
B: I thought it was fantastic. What about you?
A: I agree. I liked it too, but my sister thought it was terrible.

Exercise 4 🎧
1 Five conversations.
2 Three pictures.
3 Twice / Two times.
4 You put a tick under the right answer.

Exercise 5 🎧
1 How many people were at the meeting?
2 30.
3 There is a tick in box C.

PREPARATION   Part 1 Tapescripts

Exercise 1b) Location
1 **Girl:** I saw Michael a minute ago. He's standing opposite the bank.
  Boy: Which bank?
  Girl: The one in Station Road.
2 **Boy:** Paul is waiting for us in the High Street.
  Girl: Where exactly?
  Boy: He said he'd wait on the bench between the newsagent's and the baker's.
3 **Girl:** Where's Lucy?
  Boy: She's waiting for you in the car park.
  Girl: The one in front of the station?
  Boy: No, the big one behind Jones' supermarket.
4 **Boy:** Where are you meeting Mandy?
  Girl: She's waiting for me on the corner of High Street and Cook Street.
5 **Boy:** Is that Francesca over there?
  Girl: Where?
  Boy: Outside the sports centre.
  Girl: Yes, I think it is.
6 **Boy:** Excuse me, I have to meet my brother Sam outside the Post Office but I don't know where it is.
  Passerby: Oh, it's on High Street, next to the bank. If you walk straight on you can't miss it.
  Boy: Thank you very much.

Exercise 2b) Understanding directions
1 **Michael:** Can you tell me where the library is, please?
  Passerby: Yes, go straight up the road. It's on the right, opposite the sports centre.
2 **Sam:** Where's the nearest video shop, please?
  Passerby: Go along High Street. At the traffic lights, turn left into Barking Street. It's on the right hand side, next to the butcher's.
3 **Mandy:** Can you tell me the way to the cinema, please?
  Passerby: Go straight down here. Take the first turning on your right. You will see it in front of you at the end of the street.

EXAM PRACTICE   Part 1 Key

1 C, **2** C, **3** A, **4** B, **5** A

EXAM PRACTICE   Part 1 Tapescript

Look at the instructions for Part 1. You will hear five short conversations. You will hear each conversation twice. There is one question for each conversation. For questions 1–5, put a tick under the right answer. Here is an example:

How many people were at the meeting?
Woman: Did many people come to the meeting?
Man: About thirty.
Woman: That's quite a lot.
Man: Yes, more than last time.

The answer is thirty, so there is a tick in box C. Now we are ready to start. Look at question one.

1 *Where will the man and woman meet?*
Woman: So I'll meet you at seven thirty outside the cinema, right?
Man: No, not there. Let's meet in front of the bank.
Woman: The bank opposite the fish and chip shop?
Man: Yes, that's the one.
Woman: OK, see you at seven thirty in front of the bank.
Now listen again.
[REPEAT]

2 *Which picture does the man like the most?*
Woman: Which picture do you like best? That one with the boats is good, isn't it?
Man: No, I don't like it. I love that picture of the village houses. It's beautiful.
Woman: Yes, it's not bad, but that one over there is really great. Look at those animals!
Man: No, I don't agree.
Now listen again.

3 *What does the man ask for?*
Woman: What would you like to eat?
Man: I'll have a pizza, please.
Woman: Would you like a drink with it? Water, or some juice maybe?
Man: Mmm, yes, an orange juice, please.
Now listen again.

4 *What is the weather like now?*
Woman: Shall we go for a walk by the river?
Man: Well, I don't know. I think it may rain later.
Woman: But the sun is shining! It's a beautiful day now. There isn't a cloud in the sky!
Man: OK.
Now listen again.

5 *How many bread rolls does the woman want?*
Baker: Good afternoon, madam, can I help you?
Shopper: Hello, yes, I'd like some of those bread rolls, please.
Baker: Certainly. How many would you like?
Shopper: Hmm. I think six will be enough.
Baker: Here you are. That's one pound fifty, please.
Now listen again.

This is the end of Part 1.

Part 2, Questions 6–10

Teacher's Notes

PREPARATION

- Before playing the recording for Exercise 2, make sure students understand *ground floor* and *first floor*. Elicit where the front door is – an arrow points to it in the diagram – and where the stairs are – these are shown by a ladder symbol. An arrow shows the top of the stairs on the first floor.
- Elicit further items to add to the list in Exercise 2b⟩.
- Exercise 3 revises colours. Elicit more colours from the students to describe their clothes or things in the classroom.
- For further practice, ask students to describe their own house and the colour scheme in each room.

PREPARATION   Part 2 Key

Exercise 1
1 Five questions.
2 Giulia and Franco.
3 Giulia's parents' house.
4 Rooms and Colours.
5 Eight colours (three more than the number of questions).
6 Twice.
7 In the box next to each room.

Exercise 2
a⟩ 🎧

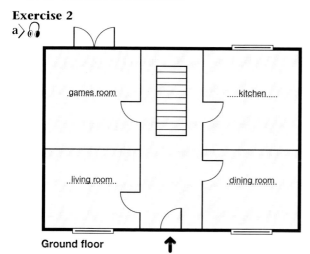

Ground floor

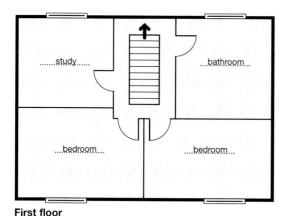

First floor

b⟩ dining room: chairs, dining table
living room: armchair, sofa   kitchen: fridge, cooker
bathroom: towel, shower   bedroom: blankets, sheets

Exercise 3
a⟩ ACROSS: blue, orange, pink, brown, red
DOWN: white, green, black, grey, yellow
b⟩ 1 blue
2 eyes: blue, brown, black, green
hair: brown, red, white, black, grey
(**Note:** not yellow – we say hair is *fair* or *blonde*.)
3 orange, brown, red, yellow
4 white, grey

PREPARATION   Part 2 Tapescript

Exercise 2a⟩ Rooms of the house
OK, here's a plan of the house. Downstairs on the ground floor, there are four big rooms, as you can see. When you go in the front door, you're in the hall. The <u>dining room is on your right and the living room is on your left.</u> You go down the hall and <u>the second door on the left is the games room.</u> It leads out into the garden, so it's great in summer. Then there's the kitchen. <u>That's the second door on the right, off the hall.</u>

When you go upstairs there's a big landing at the top of the stairs. <u>The bathroom is on the right at the top of the stairs. There are two bedrooms on the first floor and they're both at the front of the house. The bigger one has its own shower. The other room is a study.</u> It's very quiet because it's at the back of the house.

On the second floor, there are two more bedrooms …

EXAM PRACTICE   Part 2 Key

6 C, **7** H, **8** G, **9** D, **10** E

EXAM PRACTICE   Part 2 Tapescript

Listen to Giulia talking to Franco about her parents' house. They are painting the rooms. What colour is each room? For questions 6–10, write a letter A–H next to each room. You will hear the conversation twice.

Franco: Hello, Julia. Have your parents finished re-decorating your house yet?
Giulia: Hi, Franco. Well, almost. They're still painting some of the rooms. I'm going to help them this weekend.
Franco: What colours are they having?
Giulia: Well, <u>the bathroom is blue</u> …
Franco: What, like your <u>bedroom</u>? That's blue, isn't it?
Giulia: No, I didn't really like that colour. I wanted something different. <u>So I chose green for my bedroom walls.</u>
Franco: What about <u>the kitchen</u>, is it still dark red?
Giulia: Not any more! <u>We've painted it yellow.</u> But we've repainted the <u>study</u> and that's got <u>white</u> walls now.
Franco: You need lots of light for studying, don't you?
Giulia: Yes. It was brown before and it was really dark – white is better.
Franco: And <u>the dining room</u>?
Giulia: Mum and Dad have chosen <u>orange</u>. I don't like it, but they love it! And in the <u>living room we're going to have a lovely pink</u> – I think it'll look great when it's all finished.
Franco: I'm sure it will. Those dark colours everywhere weren't very nice.

Now listen again.

This is the end of Part 2.

Part 3, Questions 11–15

Teacher's Notes

- Use Exercise 1 to remind students about the task type.
- Play the recording once. Students compare their answers, then listen again to check and complete any missing answers.
- Exercise 5 practises functional language for making plans, which is useful for the Speaking Paper as well as Listening.

PREPARATION   Part 3 Key

Exercise 1
1 Jane and Marian.
2 Jane's American cousins.
3 By ticking the correct box.
4 Twice.

EXAM PRACTICE   Part 3 Key

11 A, **12** A, **13** B, **14** C, **15** B

EXAM PRACTICE   Part 3 Tapescript

Listen to Jane talking to her friend Marian about her American cousins. For questions 11–15, tick A, B or C. You will hear the conversation twice. Look at questions 11–15 now. You have twenty seconds.

Now listen to the conversation.

Jane: Hi Marian. My <u>American cousins</u> are arriving a day early, <u>on Sunday</u>, not Monday.
Marian: So they'll be here for an extra day?
Jane: Yes. When they arrive, shall we take them to Pizza Roma?
Marian: What a good idea!
Jane: <u>The coffee and ice cream are not very good, but they'll love the pizza.</u> After that we can go to the cinema. I heard that *Friends and Enemies* is very good.
Marian: That finished last week.
Jane: What about *Purple Rain*, or that new film, <u>*Catch a Train*? Yes, let's get tickets for that.</u>
Marian: OK, I think they'll enjoy that.
Jane: What about a boat trip on Tuesday morning? Isn't there an <u>early boat at half past eight</u>?
Marian: Yes, but won't that be too early?
Jane: Maybe. There's a boat at eleven thirty, which returns at about half past one.
Marian: Fine. What about Wednesday?
Jane: Well, on Wednesday we can go to the sea. Shall we go on our bicycles?
Marian: Well, it's cheaper than going by bus! And the train is so slow.
Jane: OK, <u>so let's take our bicycles.</u>

This is the end of Part Three.

Exercise 5 🎧
a⟩ 'What about' (followed by a verb in the *-ing* form)
  'I'd rather' (followed by bare infinitive)
  'Why don't we' (followed by bare infinitive)
  'Shall we' (followed by bare infinitive)

'Do you want' (followed by a *to* infinitive)
'Let's' (followed by bare infinitive)

Exercise 5 Tapescript
See Students' Book page 70 and Answer Key above.

Part 4, Questions 16–20

Teacher's Notes

PREPARATION

- Use Exercise 1 to remind students about the task.
- Exercises 2–4 revise parts of the body and vocabulary related to health.
  Note: Anagrams can easily be designed to give spelling practice in all topic areas.
- Encourage students always to try and predict the **type** of answer that is needed (Exercise 5).
- Point out that if a word is spelled on the recording (question 16), they must spell it correctly in their answer.

PREPARATION   Part 4 Key

Exercise 1
1 Five questions.
2 A woman talking to a doctor.
3 How the woman is feeling.
4 On the form.
5 Twice.

Exercise 2
1 ears, 2 nose, 3 wrist, 4 mouth / stomach, 5 ankle, 6 teeth

Exercise 3
a⟩ 1 temperature, 2 headache, 3 toothache, 4 cough, 5 pain
b⟩ 1 Mario should take an aspirin.
  2 Christine should go to the dentist.
  3 Joe should see a doctor.
  4 Susan should stay in bed.
  5 Alison should take some medicine for it.

PREPARATION   Part 4 Tapescript

Exercise 4⟩ Health
1 **Woman:** Susan's got a temperature.
  Man: She should stay in bed.
2 **Man:** Mario's got a headache.
  Woman: He should take an aspirin.
3 **Woman:** Christine is at home because she's got a bad toothache.
  Man: She should go to the dentist.
4 **Man:** Alison has got a terrible cough.
  Woman: She should take some medicine for it.
5 **Woman:** Joe can't go out today. He's got a pain in his chest.
  Man: He should see the doctor.

EXAM PRACTICE   Part 4 Key

16 NOPAIN, **17** 2 / two, **18** eating / meals / food, **19** 5 / five, **20** 2nd September OR 2/9

You will hear a woman talking to a doctor about how she is feeling. Listen and complete questions 16–20. You will hear the conversation twice.

Peggy: Good afternoon, Doctor Jenkins. My name's Peggy, Peggy Jones.

Doctor: Good afternoon, Peggy. What's the problem?

Peggy: Well, I don't feel very well, doctor. I've got a terrible earache.

Doctor: I can give you a new medicine called <u>Nopain</u>, which is very good. You can get it at any chemist's.

Peggy: Nopain? How do you spell that?

Doctor: <u>N-O-P-A-I-N.</u> OK?

Peggy: How often do I have to take the medicine?

Doctor: <u>Twice a day.</u>

Peggy: Two times a day? Before or after eating?

Doctor: <u>Always afterwards</u>, that's very important.

Peggy: And how long do I have to take it for?

Doctor: You have to finish the bottle, so that's <u>five days</u>. Come back and see me then.

Peggy: Next Monday? The first of September?

Doctor: No, not Monday, Tuesday. <u>That's the second of September.</u>

Peggy: What time can I see you doctor?

Doctor: You have to make an appointment with the receptionist outside.

Peggy: Thank you very much, doctor. I'll see you on the second of September. Goodbye.

Doctor: I hope you feel better soon. Goodbye.

Now listen again.

This is the end of Part 4.

Part 5, Questions 21–25

Teacher's Notes

PREPARATION

- Use Exercises 1 and 2 to get students to read the instructions to the exam task and predict the type of information that is missing.
- Sports vocabulary may be tested in the exam. Exercises 3–4 revise useful vocabulary.
- For Exercise **3b**〉, elicit more sports to add to each column.
- Exercises **3c**〉 and **d**〉 are useful practice for the Speaking Test. Point out the collocations: **play** (*ball games*); **go** *climbing, swimming, sailing, hang gliding;* **do** *judo, gymnastics, aerobics,* etc.
- Exercise 4 revises names of sports in a format similar to Reading Part 2, Questions 11–15. Tell students the sports are all from Exercise 3.

PREPARATION   Part 5 Key

Exercise 1

1 Five questions.   2 Information about a sports centre.
3 On the form.   4 Twice.

Exercise 2

21 times, 22 a sport, 23 a price, 24 a date, 25 a telephone number

Exercise 3

a〉 1 rock climbing, 2 swimming, 3 table tennis, 4 ice hockey, 5 judo, 6 sailing, 7 gymnastics, 8 hang gliding

b〉

ball games		water sports	adventure sports	other individual sports
individual	team	swimming	mountain climbing	judo
table tennis	ice hockey	sailing	hang gliding	gymnastics

c〉 1 play, 2 gone, 3 do

Exercise 4

1 table tennis, 2 ice hockey, 3 judo, 4 sailing, 5 gymnastics

EXAM PRACTICE   Part 5 Key

21 9 / nine a.m. to 7 / seven p.m., **22** football, **23** 50 / fifty, **24** 29 May / 29th May, **25** 432 1904 (four three two, one nine oh four)

EXAM PRACTICE   Part 5

You will hear some information about a sports centre. Listen and complete questions 21–25. You will hear the information twice.

Hello. This is a recorded message from the Cambridge Sports Centre. There is nobody here to speak to you right now, but please listen to this important information.

The centre is open Monday to Friday from eight o'clock in the morning until ten at night and from <u>nine o'clock in the morning until seven in the evening on Saturdays and Sundays</u>.

Many sports are available here, for example, basketball, tennis and <u>football</u>. You don't need your own equipment, because we have equipment for hire.

If you buy <u>a six-month season ticket for fifty pounds</u>, we have a special gift for you. With your six-month ticket, we will give you a free T-shirt from our new sports clothes shop.

From Monday the twenty-second of May, the sports centre is closed for one week. <u>We will be open again on Monday the twenty-ninth of May.</u>

From the twenty-ninth of May, we will have a new telephone number. Please call us on Cambridge four three two, one nine oh four. Thank you for calling the Cambridge Sports Centre. See you soon!

This is the end of Part 5.

Test 2

Paper 3   Speaking

Part 1

Teacher's Notes

- Exercises 1–2 give students more guided practice in asking and answering questions of the type they may be asked in the exam.
- Tell students to read the conversation in Exercise **1a**〉 before playing the recording. Point out that the

alternative answers are both grammatically accurate and appropriate. They give students an idea of the range of answers possible. Listening to the recording is useful for pronunciation. Students should then practise giving answers that are true for them.

- Exercise 2 revises past and future tenses in the context of the Speaking Test. Again, students should practise answering the questions with reference to their own experience.
- For the exam task, the questions are on the recording. Put students into pairs, A and B. Play the questions for Student A, pausing after each question. Student A should address his/her answers to Student B. Then do the same for Student B's questions.

PREPARATION   Part 1 Key

Exercise 1 🎧
a⟩ a), b), b), a)

Exercise 2 🎧
a⟩ had, came, danced, had, stayed, went, did, are going to go, to be

PREPARATION   Part 1 Tapescripts

See Students' Book page 76 and Answer key above.

EXAM PRACTICE   Part 1 Key

Answers will vary.

EXAM PRACTICE   Part 1 Tapescript

You will hear an examiner asking some questions.
Candidate A, listen carefully and answer the questions.

Examiner:
What school do you go to?
How long have you been there?
What do you like about your home town?
What other country would you most like to visit?
Did you do anything interesting last weekend?
Thank you.

You will hear an examiner asking some questions.
Candidate B, listen carefully and answer the questions.

Examiner:
What do you think of your home town?
Have you been to any other countries?
Where did you go last holiday?
What are your plans for the weekend?
What do you want to do when you finish school?
Thank you.

Part 2

Teacher's Notes

PREPARATION

- Exercise 1 introduces the type of prompt cards used to cue questions and answers of a non-personal kind, in this case about a children's museum.
- Exercise 2 gives guided practice in asking appropriate and accurate questions based on B's prompt card. After checking answers as a class, let students practise asking and answering the questions in open or closed pairs.

- For the exam practice, make sure students know where to find the cards with the information to answer the questions (they are at the back of the Students' Book).
- You could time students, giving them only two minutes to ask and answer questions for each prompt card without preparation, to simulate exam conditions.

PREPARATION   Part 2 Key

Exercise 1
1 A has some information about a museum.
2 B does not have this information.
3 B has to ask A some questions about the museum.
4 There is no need to write anything.

Exercise 2
a⟩ See tapescript.

PREPARATION   Part 2 Tapescript

Exercise 2a⟩ Making questions
What can you see at the Children's Museum?
Is it open on Sundays?
Can you buy anything to eat and drink there?
How can I get there?
How much does it cost?

EXAM PRACTICE   Part 2 Key

CD MARKET – Possible questions and answers
What's the address of the CD Market?
Sixty-eight High Street.
Is it large or small?
It's the biggest CD market in the country. / It's very big.
Is it closed on Saturdays?
No, it's open from nine a.m. to nine p.m. on Saturdays.
What kind of music do they sell?
Rock music.
What's the telephone number?
Six seven eight, five four three.

YOUTH CLUB – Possible questions and answers
Who is the club for?
For under seventeens and over twelves.
What days is it open?
Every Friday and Saturday.
How much does it cost?
Only two pound fifty per week.
What can you do there?
You can dance, listen to music or play games.
Where is it?
It's in Cambridge Street. / The address is eighty-nine, Cambridge Street.

Test 3

Reading and Writing

Part 1, Questions 1–5

1 D, 2 F, 3 B, 4 G, 5 C

Part 2, Questions 6–10

6 B, 7 C, 8 B, 9 C, 10 A

Part 3, Questions 11–15

11 A, 12 B, 13 C, 14 C, 15 A

Part 3, Questions 16–20

16 H, 17 A, 18 B, 19 F, 20 D

Part 4, Questions 21–27

21 B, 22 B, 23 C, 24 A, 25 B, 26 A, 27 B

Part 5, Questions 28–35

28 A, 29 B, 30 A, 31 C, 32 C, 33 B, 34 A, 35 B

Part 6, Questions 36–40

36 chocolate, 37 milk, 38 tomato, 39 salt, 40 vegetable

Part 7, Questions 41–50

41 is, 42 been, 43 it, 44 went, 45 are, 46 some, 47 take, 48 on / up, 49 the, 50 you

Part 8, Questions 51–55

51 Pelucci, 52 Vittoria, 53 (1 football) shirt, 54 white, 55 small

Part 9, Question 56

Sample answer (28 words)

> Hi (name)!
> I am going to the CD shop and the bookshop. I am going to buy a present for my brother's birthday. I will be back at six / 6 o'clock.
> See you soon.
> Bye,
> (name)

Listening

Part 1, Questions 1–5

1 A, 2 C, 3 B, 4 A, 5 C

Part 1 Tapescript

Look at the instructions for Part One. You will hear five short conversations. You will hear each conversation twice. There is one question for each conversation. For questions 1–5, put a tick under the right answer.
Here is an example:

What time is it?
Woman: Excuse me, can you tell me the time?
Man: Yes, it's <u>nine o'clock</u>.
Woman: Thank you.
Man: You're welcome.

The answer is nine o'clock, so there is a tick in box C.
Now we are ready to start. Look at question 1.

1 *Where is Mark going at the weekend?*
Woman: What are you doing this weekend, Mark?
Mark: Well, I wanted to go to the mountains or the forest, but I've got no one to go with.
Woman: <u>I'm going to the river. Do you want to come with me?</u>
Mark: <u>Thanks! Great!</u>

2 *How many students are there at the school?*
Woman: Last year there were six hundred students at the school.
Man: Really? Are there more this year?
Woman: Yes, there are one hundred more this year.
Teacher: So now there are <u>seven hundred</u>?
Man: Yes, that's right.

3 *Where is the hospital?*
Woman: Can you tell me the way to the hospital?
Man: Yes. <u>Go down this street and take the second road on your left.</u>
Woman: Is that before or after the traffic lights?
Man: It's <u>just before the lights</u>.

4 *What must they remember to take?*
Wife: OK, so we've got our passports.
Husband: Yes, and we've got our plane tickets and traveller's cheques.
Wife: Have we forgotten anything?
Husband: Umm, yes, <u>we must remember to take some film for the camera.</u>

5 *Which is Christina's family?*
Boy: Your brother is much taller than you, isn't he, Christina?
Girl: <u>No, he's shorter.</u>
Boy: And <u>your father, what about him?</u>
Girl: Well, <u>I'm shorter than him.</u>

This is the end of Part 1.

Part 2

6 C, 7 E, 8 B, 9 A, 10 H

Now look at Part 2. Listen to Mario talking to Francesca about his birthday presents. What presents did each person give Mario? For questions 6–10, write a letter A–H next to each person. You will hear the conversation twice.

Francesca: Hello, Mario. I really enjoyed your birthday party.
Mario: Did you? Good!
Francesca: What presents did you get? Did Dinos buy you a T-shirt?
Mario: No, he didn't! He bought me a sweater and Paul gave me a computer book.
Francesca: What about your mum and dad?
Mario: They're paying for me to go on holiday to the USA next summer! Can you believe it?!
Francesca: Hey, that's great, Mario. What about your sister?
Mario: Well, usually she gives me something really boring, like socks, but this year she gave me a Walkman.
Francesca: Wow! And I'm sure your uncle in Australia sent you something expensive as always.
Mario: Yes, Uncle Terry sent me a great bag for college, you know, the kind you wear over your shoulder?
Francesca: That was a good idea for a present, wasn't it? Anything else?
Mario: No, that's everything. Wait a minute, I found a watch, but I don't know who it's from!
Francesca: That was from me!
Mario: Oops, sorry! Thank you, Francesca.

Now listen again.

This is the end of Part 2.

Part 3

11 B, **12** A, **13** B, **14** B, **15** C

Now look at Part 3. Listen to Stephanie talking to an assistant at the chemist's about her photographs. For questions 11–15, tick A, B or C. You will hear the conversation twice. Look at questions 11–15 now. You have twenty seconds.

Now listen to the conversation.

Assistant: Good morning, madam. Can I help you?
Stephanie: Yes, I left two films here last Monday for developing and I've come to get my photographs.
Assistant: Have you got your ticket?
Stephanie: No, I'm afraid I couldn't find it. I'm very sorry.
Assistant: Never mind. What's your name, please?
Stephanie: Stephanie Philips. That's P-H-I-L-I-P-S.
Assistant: Thank you. Let me see. Here we are, Ms Philips. Please check to see if the photos are all right.
Stephanie: Oh dear, some of them aren't too bad, but these are very dark, aren't they?
Assistant: Yes, the problem is you took those photos with the sun in front of you. The sun should be behind you.
Stephanie: And why are the people in these photos so small?
Assistant: Well, you took them from too far away.
Stephanie: Is there anything I've done right?
Assistant: Yes! Some of your photos are very beautiful … the river here, those animals.

Stephanie: Oh, thank you!
Assistant: You're welcome. Oh, by the way, that's nine pounds ninety-nine.
Stephanie: Of course, here you are.
Assistant: Thank you.

Now listen again.

This is the end of Part 3.

Part 4

16 Supermarket, **17** 5.15, (five pounds, fifteen), **18** RUBINO, **19** half past five / five thirty / 5.30 p.m., **20** post office

Now look at Part 4. You will hear a student telephoning about a weekend job. Listen and complete questions 16–20. You will hear the conversation twice.

Woman: Good afternoon, Lo-Price Supermarket. Can I help you?
Student: Yes, please. I saw your advertisement and I want to know about the weekend job.
Woman: Well, we need somebody downstairs, to lift heavy things. Have you done that before?
Student: Yes, I have and I'm very strong. How much do you pay?
Woman: Are you eighteen yet?
Student: No, I'll be eighteen next year.
Woman: We pay five pounds fifteen per hour, but six pounds thirty when you're eighteen. Can you work in the evenings, or only at the weekends?
Student: I'm a student so I can only work at the weekends.
Woman: That's not a problem. Can you come here at five o'clock today to meet the manager? Her name is Mrs Rubino.
Student: I'm sorry?
Woman: Mrs Rubino. R-U-B-I-N-O.
Student: I have a class until five, but I can be there a little later.
Woman: OK, come at five thirty then.
Student: Alright. Where is the supermarket, please?
Woman: It's next to the post office in the High Street.
Student: Thank you.

Now listen again.

This is the end of Part 4.

Part 5

21 eight thirty / half past eight / 8.30 a.m., **22** 10 / ten, **23** the office, **24** 8 / eight, **25** food

Now look at Part 5. You will hear some information about buses to London. Listen and complete questions 21–25. You will hear the information twice.

Hello. This is a recorded message from Yellow Buses. Our office is closed at the moment. We open again on Monday morning <u>at eight thirty</u> and close at seven o'clock in the evening. On Sunday the office is open from nine a.m. to six p.m.

There are <u>ten buses to London each day</u>. They leave the bus station at thirty minutes past each hour. On Sunday there are seven buses. The journey to London takes about two hours.

You can <u>buy tickets when this office is open</u>, or on the bus when you travel. Return tickets cost fifteen pounds for an adult and <u>eight pounds for children and students</u>. Single tickets cost eleven pounds and five pounds for children and students.

<u>Food</u> and drink are for sale on the bus. Sandwiches cost one pound ninety and orange juice costs seventy-five pence. Coffee and tea cost one pound ten.

Thank you for calling Yellow Buses.

Now listen again.

This is the end of Part 5.

You now have eight minutes to write your answers on the answer sheet. Now pause the tape. This is the end of the test.

TEST 4

Reading

Part 1, Questions 1–5
1 B, **2** D, **4** A, **5** G, **6** H

Part 2, Questions 6–10
6 A, **7** C, **8** C, **9** C, **10** A

Part 3, Questions 11–15
11 A, **12** C, **13** B, **14** C, **15** B

Part 3, Questions 16–20
16 H, **17** A, **18** B, **19** G, **20** C

Part 4, Questions 21–27
21 A, **22** C, **23** B, **24** A, **25** C, **26** B, **27** A

Part 5, Questions 28–35
28 A, **29** B, **30** C, **31** A, **32** B, **33** C, **34** A, **35** B

Part 6, Questions 36–40
36 telephone, **37** cupboard, **38** bowl, **39** glass, **40** towel

Part 7, Questions 41–50
41 to, **42** has, **43** go, **44** he, **45** give / bring, **46** unwell / ill / sick, **47** will / can, **48** him, **49** for, **50** better

Part 8, Questions 51–55
51 Bradbury, **52** 1 / one, **53** London, **54** coach, **55** 1,500 (one thousand, five hundred)

Part 9, Question 56
Sample answer (27 words)

> Hi Roberto!
> I'm sorry. Yes, I have still got your CD player. I can return it to you on Friday. Please can I borrow it again next week?
> Bye,
> (name)

Listening

Part 1, Questions 1–5
1 C, **2** C, **3** A, **4** B, **5** A

Look at the instructions for Part 1. You will hear five short conversations. You will hear each conversation twice. There is one question for each conversation. For questions 1–5, put a tick under the right answer.
Here is an example:
How many people were at the meeting?
Woman: Did many people come to the meeting?
Man: <u>About thirty.</u>
Woman: That's quite a lot.
Man: Yes, more than last time.

The answer is thirty, so there is a tick in box C.
Now we are ready to start. Look at question one.

1 *How much was the restaurant bill?*
Woman: How much did the meal cost?
Man: I think <u>it was fifty pounds all together</u>.
Woman: That's very expensive for two people ... twenty-five pounds each.
Man: Yes, but the food was very good.
Now listen again.
[REPEAT]

2 *How long was the journey?*
Woman: What time did the boat leave?
Man: Early in the morning, at six o'clock.
Woman: And you arrived at ten in the evening?
Man: Yes, so we were on the boat <u>for sixteen hours</u>!
Now listen again.

3 *What did the man do last night?*
Female: So, what did you do last night?
Male: Well, I was thinking of going to the cinema or the theatre.
Female: But you didn't go? Why's that?
Male: <u>I was tired so I stayed at home and watched television.</u>
Now listen again.

4 *How does Stefano usually get to school?*
Woman: Do you walk to school every day, Stefano?
Man: <u>No, my brother takes me in his car.</u>
Woman: So where's your brother today?
Man: He's on a bus – his car isn't working!
Now listen again.

5 *How did she hear about the accident?*
Man: Did you hear about the accident in the newspaper?
Woman: No, it wasn't in the paper and it wasn't on the radio either. <u>My sister told me about it when she phoned me.</u>
Man: Oh, I see …
Now listen again.

This is the end of Part 1.

Part 2, Questions 6–10

6 F, **7** A, **8** G, **9** H, **10** B

Part 2 Tapescript

Listen to David talking to Isabel about his family. Where did each person go on Saturday? For questions 6–10, write a letter A–H next to each person. You will hear the conversation twice.

Isabel: Hello, David. Did you have a good weekend?
David: Hi, Isabel. Yes, but I was very busy.
Isabel: What did you do?
David: Well, on <u>Saturday morning I had to take Emily to the dentist because she had a toothache.</u>
Isabel: Oh, dear! Is she alright now?
David: Yes, she's OK. After the dentist I had <u>to drive my father to the supermarket.</u> He doesn't like shopping alone and he wanted me to help him buy the food for dinner.
Isabel: Did you <u>go to the game</u> in the afternoon?
David: I didn't have time, but <u>Sara went – she thinks basketball is great.</u> I <u>took Rob swimming</u> at three o'clock, but we were late because of the traffic.
Isabel: Where was <u>Ricky</u>?
David: <u>He went to his lesson at the tennis club.</u>
Isabel: Was your <u>mother</u> at home alone?
David: Only until about six o'clock and then I had <u>to take her to see that new Tom Cruise film</u>! It was quite good!

Now listen again.

This is the end of Part 2.

Part 3, Questions 11–15

11 B, **12** C, **13** B, **14** C, **15** A

Part 3 Tapescript

Listen to Anna talking to her friend Sarah about a summer job. For questions 11–15, tick A, B or C. You will hear the conversation twice. Look at questions 11–15 now. You have twenty seconds.

Now listen to the conversation.

Anna: Double five seven, three four one two, hello.
Sarah: Is that Anna? Sarah here. How are you?

Part 3 Tapescript

Anna: Hi, Sarah, I'm OK, but I'm looking for a summer holiday job.
Sarah: Are you? <u>My dad needs another assistant in his shop.</u>
Anna: Working with you? Tell me something about the job.
Sarah: Well, it's full-time, five days a week.
Anna: What time do you start work in the morning?
Sarah: <u>At eight o'clock.</u> I usually get the bus at seven thirty.
Anna: Hmm, OK. And what's the pay? I want to save some money for a new computer game.
Sarah: Well, <u>I get four pounds fifty an hour</u>, but for the first month you'll get four pounds. Some people get five pounds.
Anna: Is there somewhere to eat near the shop, or do you take something from home for your lunch?
Sarah: <u>Most days I take sandwiches</u> from home. <u>There's a park around the corner and I usually eat them in the park.</u> But sometimes I go to Pizza Roma.
Anna: Perhaps I'll go to see your dad. Where's the shop exactly?
Sarah: It's in <u>Byronos Avenue – B-Y-R-O-N-O-S.</u>
Anna: Thanks, Sarah. Goodbye. Wish me luck!

Now listen again.

This is the end of Part 3.

Part 4, Questions 16–20

16 Monday, **17** August, **18** eight thirty / half past eight / 8.30, **19** 158 (one hundred and fifty-eight), **20** railway

Part 4 Tapescript

You will hear a student telephoning a school. Listen and complete questions 16–20. You will hear the conversation twice.

Woman: Good afternoon, Crown English Language School.
Student: Hello. Can you give me some information about your school?
Woman: Yes, of course. How can I help you?
Student: First, when does the next English class begin?
Woman: We always start a new class on the first <u>Monday</u> of each month. So, the next class begins on Monday <u>the fourth of August</u> – that's next week.
Student: Good. What time do the classes begin?
Woman: Well, they start at <u>eight thirty</u>, but on the first day students need to come a little earlier, at about a quarter past eight.
Student: And where is the school? I don't have the address.
Woman: The school is at the end of Bridge Road, number <u>one hundred and fifty eight</u>, on the left.
Student: Let me look on my map … just a minute …
Woman: We're just <u>next to the railway station</u>.
Student: OK, I've got it. Thank you very much for all your help.
Woman: You're welcome. Goodbye.
Student: Goodbye.

Now listen again.

This is the end of Part 4.

Part 5, Questions 21–25

21 Monday, **22** one / 1, **23** 8 / eight, **24** April,
25 8390 42 75 (eight three nine oh, four two, seven five)

Extra practice

Exercise 1
a) 1 notice, 2 comic, 3 timetable, 4 postcard,
  5 magazine, 6 newspaper
b) 1 photographer, 2 baker, 3 mechanic, 4 receptionist,
  5 doctor, 6 tourists, 7 pilot, 8 travel agent's

Exercise 2
a) **Holidays:** passport, suitcase, guest, journey, ticket, museum, tour guide
  School: classroom, desk, lesson, computer, teacher, homework, library
  World: planet, earth, rain forest, plants, scientist, zoo, sunshine
b) **Holidays:** 1 guests, 2 suitcase, 3 tickets, 4 journey
  School: 1 homework, 2 library, 3 desk, 4 classroom
  World: 1 zoo, 2 rain forest, 3 plants, 4 scientist

Exercise 3
a) 1 passenger, 2 dangerous, 3 plastic, 4 temperature,
  5 square, 6 marmalade, 7 sweater, 8 Thursday,
  9 breakfast, 10 theatre, 11 dictionary,
  12 (**possible answer**) A big shop where you can buy food and drinks, as well as many other things.
b) **People:** passenger, (**possible answers:** scientist, guest, tour guide)

Days of the week: Thursday, (**possible answers:** Tuesday, Wednesday, Friday)
Food and meals: marmalade, breakfast, (**possible answers:** lunch, dinner, bread)
Shapes and materials: square, plastic, (**possible answers:** rectangle, leather, wood)
Clothes: sweater, (**possible answers:** jacket, skirt, shirt)
Health: temperature, (**possible answers:** headache, toothache, pain)
Places: theatre, supermarket, (**possible answers:** sports centre, school, airport)
No group: dictionary, dangerous

Exercise 4
1 to, 2 at, 3 on, 4 in, 5 at, 6 On, 7 at, 8 in, 9 to, 10 on

Exercise 5
a) 1 to / by, 2 by, 3 to, 4 to, 5 in, 6 in / on, 7 in, 8 from

Exercise 6
1 My school is called St John's.
2 I have two sisters and one brother. / I have one brother and two sisters.
3 What do you usually do at weekends?
4 My favourite food is hamburger and chips.
5 Where did you go on holiday last year?
6 What kind of books do you like best?

Exercise 7
a) 1 but, 2 so, 3 because, 4 and, 5 or, 6 so
b) because / and / or / but / so

Exercise 8
a) 1 Ryan Giggs, the famous Manchester United footballer, was born in 1973.
  2 The first team he played for was Manchester City.
  3 Giggs also plays for his country, Wales.
  4 He first played for Wales when he was only 17 years old.
  5 Giggs has also been the captain of the Welsh team.
  6 He likes swimming, hang gliding and reading.
b) <u>We</u>'ll be in Bournemouth tomorrow at six o'clock<u>. C</u>an we meet you<u>? W</u>hat time will you be free<u>? S</u>hall we bring our swimming things with us<u>? I</u>'ll call you when we arrive<u>.</u>

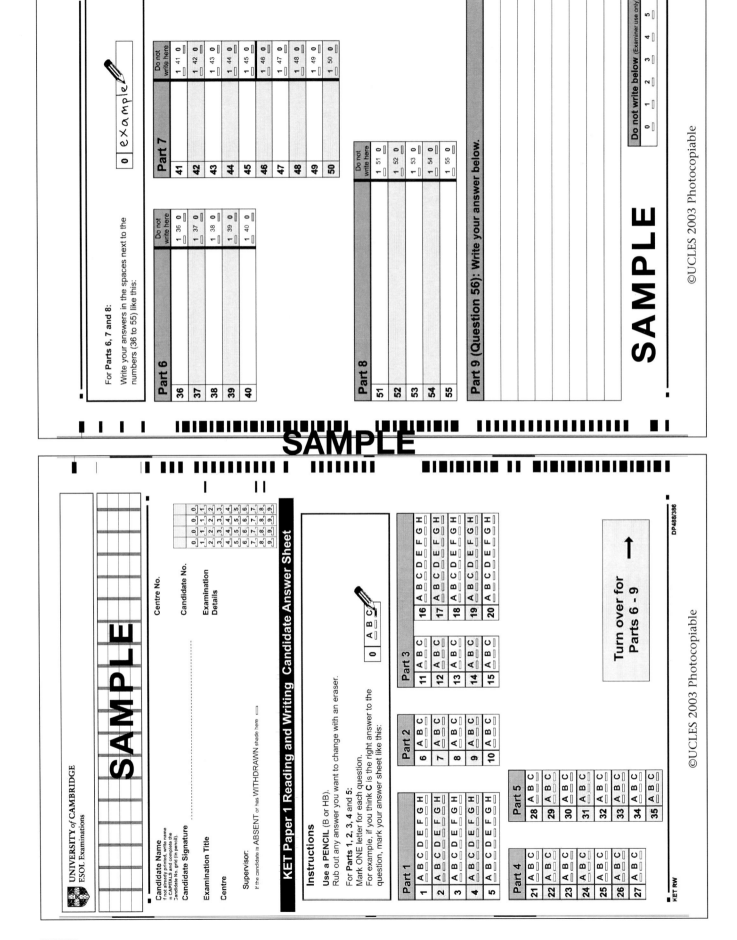